Disclaimer and FTC Notice

While all attempts have been made to verify the information provided in this publication, neither the author nor the publisher assumes any responsibility for errors, omissions, or contrary interpretations of the subject matter herein. This book is for entertainment purposes only. The views expressed are those of the author alone, and should not be taken as expert instruction or commands. The reader is responsible for his or her own actions.

Adherence to all applicable laws and regulations, including international, federal, state, and local governing professional licensing, business practices, advertising, and all other aspects of

Introduction

Self-help books are bullshit. We've all read them. We've all hoped for that one special book ripe with information that actually works. The magic bullet.

Unfortunately, most of these self-help turds don't live up to the hype. And not just that. Most take hundreds of pages to get to the point.

We do GET THE POINT. The point is providing substance— not a salacious mental masturbation. Give me gold nuggets, or give me death!

The problem is the popular. We all want to *Think and Grow Rich*. We all want *The Secret*. *The Secret* to manifest our dreams.

The secret is simple. You know the secret. I know the secret. The secret is to act—*Act and Grow Rich*.

Who Should Read This Book?

Don't read this book if you only think, but don't act. Don't read this book if you are lazy. If you are happy with mediocre, stop now. This book is not for the average.

As a lifetime student of personal habits, mindset, productivity, and ACTION, we've read and tested hundreds of the best books and articles on the subject of success.

By reading this book, you will be in the top 10% of achievers. Instead of wishing for your dreams, you will act your dreams into existence.

We promise that if you follow everything in this book and ACT, you'll be RICH both personally and professionally. And, we will teach you to think rich.

Don't be the person who misses out on opportunities in life because you fail to act. Be the kind of person that others envy. Be the kind of person that people say, "Everything they touch turns to gold."

The tips and tricks you are about to read will take your life to the next level. New level. New you.

ACT.

Act and Grow Rich.

Directives

The Only Productivity Guide You Will Ever Need

Each night, when I go to sleep, I die. And the next morning, when I wake up, I am reborn.

—Mahatma Gandhi

* * *

Below are the best productivity tips I've learned. My hope is to save you not only money, but your most valuable commodity—time. Enjoy.

❖ Answer emails that require less than 5 minutes of attention immediately.

❖ Complete tasks coming in that take 5 minutes or less, immediately.

❖ Refuse to setup your voicemail (I personally never check voicemail. The sky still isn't falling).

❖ Increase your computer mouse speed to as fast as possible.

❖ Use at least two monitors at work.

❖ Set up calendar reminders for tasks requiring attention on a daily, weekly, monthly, or quarterly basis.

❖ De-clutter your brain from having to remember anything.

❖ Use Brian Tracy's [1] 45-file folder system for organization—45 file folders (12 for months, 31 for days of the month, and 2 for the next two years). In the file for the day, put tasks you want to work on. Check folders each day. Never again worry about forgetting something. Most importantly, get rid of the cognitive load you put on yourself when trying to remember anything and everything. You can't and you won't.

❖ Each day, work on highest priority (most pain in the ass) task first—otherwise, you won't do it. Refer to Brian Tracy's *Eat That Frog!*

❖ Establish daily habits that done only several days in a row wouldn't make much of a difference, but done on a monthly or longer cycle would make drastic changes, e.g., reading 10 pages every day of work literature. Refer to *The Slight Edge* by Jeff Olson.

❖ Avoid time-wasting meetings at all costs.

❖ If given the option for email or phone call, take the less time-consuming of the two:

Scenario 1: If a person wants to tell you how adorable their new cockatoo is—email

Scenario 2: If a person is a tight-lipped Tommy—call

❖ If possible, batch tasks together. 12-1 pm: phone calls, 3-4 pm: emails. Refer to Tim Ferriss' book *The 4-Hour Workweek.*

❖   If able, delegate any tasks below your hourly wage, i.e., "Is this a $25 task?" If below the threshold, delegate to others.

❖   At the end of each work day, clear your desk of ALL clutter—only leaving the file with the next day's tasks in it.

❖   Take mini 10 minute breaks after 50 minutes of work. Research shows this increases productivity.

❖   If you want written documentation of something, email. Someone's word over the phone can "change."

❖   Keep all emails. Archive. If someone sends you notification of non-receipt, kindly forward them previously sent email. They will appreciate it. You will appreciate the e-win.

❖   Don't email large attachments. As my boss says, "For Pete's sake, a 4 MB file!"

❖   Get up at least one to two hours before leaving for work and follow Hal Elrod's advice from *The Miracle Morning.* At a minimum, get in 10 minutes of meditation, 10 minutes of reading, 10 minutes of affirmations, 10 minutes of visualization, 10 minutes of journaling, and 10 minutes of exercise.

Management for Morons: A Primer

Always bear in mind that your own resolution to succeed is more important than any other one thing.

—Abraham Lincoln

* * *

Thou shalt lead by exception. Define task; have employee repeat back to you; set deadline and criteria; leave alone; leave alone; help if asked; leave alone; check results on deadline date.

❖ Thou shalt not include the prefix micro before the word manage. Micromanaging doesn't work.

❖ Thou shalt be sociable. Depending on the day, this may or may not begin until after 10 or 11 a.m.

❖ Thou shalt hire people smarter than you.

❖ Thou shalt ask your employees about their lives. If you care about them, they'll care about you. Find out how Paul's pet chinchilla is doing. Oh, Jennifer had a root canal? Ask her about it. Pete likes bowling? Ask him about his bowling league. Carla likes competitive cat grooming? Well…Some things are better left unsaid.

❖   Thou shalt use co-worker's first names when addressing them. "Hey you," is not an acceptable salutation. It's Karen. It's Steve. It's Johnny Jenkins.

❖   Thou shalt do as you say and say as you do.

❖   Thou shalt complete tasks capable of being completed within 5 minutes on a FIFO-basis—first in, first out.

❖   Thou shalt only lookout the window a maximum of three times. Don't let your subordinates catch you gloating about your great view. Cubicle nation is stronger than the best of unions—excluding Walmart, because they just don't give a shit about your stupid union-talk.

❖   Thou shalt use a stern face >:O when being managerial-like.

❖   Thou shalt use a smiley face :-D when being buddy-like (when you want them getting shit done).

❖   Thou shalt use a winky face ;-) NEVER. That is how lawsuits happen; you getting sued; getting called a sexist, ass-grabbing pig (in a pig's defense, I'm not sure they could grab any ass with those little nubs for hands)

❖   Thou shalt never set up your voicemail. Make them email you. This is the twenty-first century.

❖   Thou shalt keep meetings to a maximum of once per day—the 15-30 minutes required for bathroom reading time, or as I like to call it "self-improvement time."

❖ Thou shalt include a witty quote from a past president or some other witticism from another historical figure in your email signature block. Everyone loves a good quote.

"If It's Not a Fuck Yes, It's a Fuck No."

No is a complete sentence. It does not require justification or explanation.

—Anonymous

* * *

24 hours. Every day. The only limitation in life is time. Bill Gates has 24 hours. Warren Buffett has 24 hours. You have 24 hours. Every day. I have 24 hours every day. No more. No less. While many of us set our own limitations in life, just realize that all of them are bullshit. The only limitation you have is your time. When time runs out, that's a wrap. Game over. Finito. And, although many of us act like time is infinite. It is not.

How differently would you act if you knew how much time you had left on this planet? What if you had a countdown timer on your wrist? Once it hit zero, that was it. What would you change? Maybe nothing. Maybe something.

As our friend Benjamin Franklin said, "In this world, nothing can be said to be certain, except death and taxes."

Before you can learn to say yes, you need to learn how to say NO. Everyone can and does say yes. Though, it's not until you start saying no that you can begin saying yes to what you want. Oh, you hate meetings? Stop going to them. Oh, you hate telemarketers? Stop answering calls from unknown callers and make them leave a voicemail if it's important. You hate your wife's meatloaf? Don't be a smartass. Smile, eat that meat loaf, and tell your wife you love it. Happy wife. Happy life.

The point is elimination. Eliminate what? Eliminate anything that does not add value to your life or your work. According to the *WSJ* [2], Americans watch an average of three hours of television every day. "Big deal," you say. Let's break that down. Three hours per day multiplied by 365 days per year gives us 1,095 hours of TV watched per year. 1,095 hours per year multiplied by twenty years gives us 21,900 hours of television watched over twenty years. According to the *Organization for Economic Co-operation and Development* [3], the average U.S. worker averages 1,789 hours worked each year. So, in twenty years, the average American watches 12 work years worth of TV.

Now, since we're talking about the power of no. What do you think my first recommendation is to say no to? I'll give you one guess. It starts with a capital T and ends with a capital V. Put them together and what do you have? TV. See. I knew you guys were smart. Now, I'm not asking or saying you need to turn into a television celibate. Rather, cut down your total TV time by half or more. Instead of three hours. Try ninety minutes. Or, for those of you who prefer 60 minutes, there's conveniently a show out there that lasts exactly 60 minutes. It's called "60 Minutes."

Derek Sivers said it well when he said, "If it's not a hell yes, it's a hell no."

While I do like the original quote, I think it can be improved. For those of you who have virgin ears, "Earmuffs."

"If it's not a fuck yes, it's a fuck no."

Always Get Promoted First and Fastest

Practice even what seems impossible. The left hand is useless at almost everything, for lack of practice. But it guides the reins better than the right. From practice.

—Marcus Aurelius, *Meditations: A New Translation*

* * *

Magic bullets. Everyone looks for them. Rarely do we find them. Why can't someone hand us the keys to the castle. The secret.

The problem is clues are everywhere. You either A) Know what is required to attain success and don't take action or B) You don't know what action to take to become successful. Most people fall into category A.

I'm here to tell you something profound. So, profound that when you combine the two things, you will far surpass every peer around you.

1)   Do your work as quickly as humanly possible

2)   Do your work at the highest level possible

3)   Do your work as quickly and as well as is humanly possible

As mentioned on the Productivity guide, reply to every email requiring less than five minutes of your attention— IMMEDIATELY. Make a game of it. My goal is always the same. Answer the email the same minute that I receive it. If not, within five minutes. People will notice. Not only notice, but notice in a big way. People will start to comment about how you are always so fast and timely. You are taking customer service to the nth degree.

Learn how to use your computer quickly and learn every possible hotkey out there. Use dual monitors. Increase your mouse or trackpad speed to maximum. Take typing classes. Learn how to use all the Microsoft Suite products or their equivalent. Technology is your friend. Embrace it. Love it. Become the go to person in the office for computer-related questions.

Next, do your work well. Not only must you perform work quickly, you must also do it flawlessly. Proofread emails multiple times. Read emails out loud. Verify all numbers, figures, spelling, and grammar are accurate. Double check. Triple check. Become the person that has a 99.9%+ accuracy. Sloppy work is a sign of sloppy thinking.

And finally, the most important of all, you must combine speed with quality work.

Speed + quality work = unlimited potential

Learn to walk circles around your co-workers. Not only walk, but RUN. Run circles around them.

For example let's look at two comparable workers working in the same accounting department:

A)   Jared does work up to par. He does what is asked of him in a reasonable amount of time. He doesn't take terribly long to respond to emails—average for how long it takes most people to respond. He does his work well enough. Most of the time, Jared is error free, but occasionally he makes noticeable mistakes.

B)   Jim works up to par, as well. He does what is asked of him and does it as fast as humanly possible. He makes a game of it. He responds to most emails within five minutes or less. He makes few errors, if any, and does his job faster and better than anyone in the accounting department. You receive a response from Jim before you can even blink.

It's an obvious decision who will be considered when a larger role becomes available. It's also obvious how to get ahead at work. It doesn't matter if it's obvious. It also doesn't matter if you already know these ideas. What does matter is applying the concepts. Put them to use.

Action Step: For the next week, answer every email within five minutes. Go as fast as you can before you start making 5-10% errors.

Work quickly.

Produce quality work.

Enjoy unlimited promotion potential.

Lessons For My Children

Would the child that you were respect the man that you've become?

—Anonymous

* * *

Treat others well, regardless of how they treat you. There are enough assholes in the world; don't be one of them.

❖ Generally, try to be a good human being. Like assholes, we have enough of them and there are already too many pricks trying to fuck someone (over).

❖ Don't worry if you don't have an answer for the question: "What do you want to be when you grow up?"

❖ Don't buy a bunch of shit that doesn't earn you more money. Buy what will appreciate. Buy enough of it and when it does, you can buy all the shit your little heart desires.

❖ Be like Tyrion Lannister and "Always pay your debts."

❖ Don't smoke crack or bang prostitutes—one could be a quick death. The other, well, could make you positive—HIV positive, that is. One of the few times when being positive is a bad, bad thing.

❖   Protect your heart. Don't love blindly. Love widely. Love deeply. Most importantly, love selectively.

❖   Contribute to society. Do not become a taker. Refer to first bullet.

❖   Money IS important. Relationships are MORE important.

❖   Don't instigate fights, but if someone starts a fight with you, finish it.

❖   Travel. Travel often. It is one of the few things that can never be taken from you.

❖   Read about stoicism, particularly Marcus Aurelius: *Meditations: A New Translation*.

❖   Earn multiple streams of income. Don't tie hours worked to your earning ability.

❖   If someone is an asshole to you, simply reply with, "Are you mad?" <jedi mind trick>

❖   Read at least 10 pages of a book daily—preferably nonfiction related to your career field.

❖   Have daily habits. Never betray yourself by not doing them.

❖   Don't listen to yourself when you say you aren't worthy or can't do something. Your mind is a lying asshole—only looking out for survival—not success.

❖ Especially don't listen to others that tell you that you aren't worthy or capable. You are worthy. You are capable. **You are whatever you tell yourself you are.**

❖ Failing doesn't make you a failure.

❖ What is success? Making a difference.

Advice to my 20-year-old Self

Congratulations, Branson. I predict that you will either go to prison or become a millionaire.

—Richard Branson, *Losing My Virginity*

* * *

You don't know anything. You may never know anything. You will be lucky to know something.

❖ The most powerful thing you can ever learn in life—I am. Nothing follows. Simply, I am.

❖ Learn to respect yourself first. Others will follow shortly after.

You can't always get what you want, but if you try sometimes…You might find you get what you need.

—The Rolling Stones

❖ You think you found your soulmate. You probably did not. You found your first love. Enjoy it.

❖ The lows always seem lower. The highs never last. Tomorrow the sun will rise.

❖ You were put here for a purpose. Don't ask, "What's the meaning of life?" It's your job to figure out your meaning and act upon it.

❖ Going to college is not a golden ticket.

❖ Always give yourself 2-3 options in life. Don't put all your eggs in one basket.

❖ See the world.

❖ Less things.

❖ More experiences.

❖ Surround yourself with only the best of company. People that bring you up.

❖ Practice gratitude daily.

❖ Meditate daily.

❖ Read daily.

❖ Write daily.

❖ What are you looking forward to in the next 7 days?

❖ Other people will like you—if—you like other people.

❖ Treat everyone you meet like they are the most important person in the world. You say everything by your actions towards those in positions below you.

Personal Finance — Slow Millionaire

I'd like to live as a poor man, with lots of money.

—Pablo Picasso

* * *

Dave Ramsey's 7 baby steps. Treat debt as your enemy. Leverage at your own risk.

- ❖ **Step 1)** Save $1,000 emergency fund
- ❖ **Step 2)** Pay off debt using debt snowball

Start with the lowest debt amount and go from there. If you have two identical debt amounts, obviously pay off the higher interest rate first.

- ❖ **Step 3)** 3-6 month of expenses in savings
- ❖ **Step 4)** Invest 15% into Roth IRAs and pretax retirement
- ❖ **Step 5)** College funding for children
- ❖ **Step 6)** Pay off home early
- ❖ **Step 7)** Build wealth and give
- ❖ Save at least 10% of each paycheck. As stated before, take a note from Sir John Templeton—who saved over 50% of his

income; he became a billionaire. Causation doesn't equal correlation. Just deserves attention.

❖ Check your bank account daily—use a tool like <u>Mint</u> to aggregate all of your finances.

❖ Once you've paid debt off, spend the following: 10% education, 10% savings, 10% investments, 10% play, 10% give

❖ NEVER cosign a loan.

❖ Only use your credit card(s) online—never your debit card. Credit cards offer greater protection.

❖ Learn what your net worth is. Don't know? Assets - liabilities = net worth.

❖ Investing in stocks? Save yourself time and money (from "actively managed funds")—only invest in index funds. What are index funds? As stated by *Investopedia* [4]"An index fund is a type of mutual fund with a portfolio constructed to match or track the components of a market index, such as the Standard & Poor's 500 Index (S&P 500). An index mutual fund is said to provide broad market exposure, low operating expenses and low portfolio turnover."

❖ Know your credit score. Your lenders will. Again, refer to <u>Mint</u> or <u>Credit Karma</u>.

❖ Spend too much money on credit cards? Simple. Only use your credit card for online purchases and gasoline. You keep your account active and don't run it up every month.

❖ Ways to have more money. To become rich, you will need both:

❖ Earn more money.

❖ Spend less money or find ways to cut costs.

❖ The lottery IS NOT an investment strategy. There is a strong relationship between those who play the lottery and those in poverty.

❖ MAKE YOUR OWN LUCK. Refer to above.

❖ A car may be an "asset," but not the kind of asset you want. You want appreciating assets, not depreciating ones. As times goes by, you want assets that increase in value—cars, however shiny and pretty they are, are not appreciating and do not increase in value—certain rare makes and models, excluded.

❖ If you make $30,000/year, don't go out and buy a car that costs $25,000.

How to Become a Millionaire

Money is a good servant but a bad master.

—Sir Francis Bacon

* * *

Change your mindset permanently. Eliminate limiting beliefs. Books to read: *The Millionaire Mind* by Thomas J. Stanley and *Secrets of the Millionaire Mind* by T. Harv Eker.

❖ Create ways to generate income that don't tie your income to hours worked. If not, you will always be a slave to money. J.O.B = Just Over Broke

❖ Create income streams that can be leveraged through scale (massive amounts of people) or magnitude (increasing amount of money per sale).

❖ Real estate is always an option. It may take time to initially build up but will eventually compound after owning enough properties.

❖ Save and invest as much of your money as possible; do not fall prey to consumerism—yet. See: Sir John Templeton— saving 50% of his income and investing.

- ❖ When possible, reinvest your earnings and cash flows.

- ❖ Only buy appreciating assets: houses, education, businesses.

- ❖ Buy less depreciating assets: cars, electronics, gold-digging women.

- ❖ Know your goal. Write it down. Look at it daily. Set a deadline. If the deadline passes, set a new deadline. Create a plan for attaining it.

- ❖ Live on less.

- ❖ Spend 10% of income on education, annually.

- ❖ Track your money on a daily basis. Get a program that tracks where your money goes, see: Mint

- ❖ Invest in lawyers, accountants, quickbooks, seminars, books, videos, courses, and conferences.

- ❖ Create daily habits that over time, will compound into huge returns, i.e., reading 10 pages of job-related material every day.

- ❖ Track daily habits. If you don't track them, you won't do them. If you set too ambitious of a habit, you won't do it, e.g., working out every day for one to two hours.

- ❖ Become better with people, networking, marketing, copywriting, sales, sales, and sales.

- ❖ To create millions. Affect millions.

Habits

The Power of Habit

Because when we sit down day after day and keep grinding, something mysterious starts to happen. A process is set into motion by which, inevitably and infallibly, heaven comes to our aid. Unseen forces enlist in our cause; serendipity reinforces our purpose.

—Steven Pressfield, *The War of Art*

* * *

Tell me your habits. I'll tell you who you are. It's that simple. People wonder why they aren't successful.

The sad part is, there is no mystery.

If a film crew videotaped your life for an entire week, what would they see? Would they see you sitting on the couch after work—drinking a beer or two? Would they see you playing with your kids, spending time with your family—only to work on your own business after they fall asleep?

Right now, I'm going to challenge you to hold your habits accountable. Download any habit app you can find. Do it now. I recommend "<u>Habit List</u>." In the app, you can setup habits you have or want to track. You can setup habits on a daily, weekly, monthly, or specific day of the week. Then, you can see how well you're doing at following through on your newly established habits.

> In the first 30 years, you make your habits. For the last 30 years of your life, your habits make you.
>
> — Steve Jobs

The most important piece of the app is the accountability. Every day you mark off completed habits. And, every day, you see how well you're doing. For example, I recently created the habit of reading 10 pages of something work-related every day. Currently, I've completed 49 days in a row—equalling 490 pages read in just 49 days. Now, do you think this small little daily habit would help make you more knowledgeable in your field?

Jerry Seinfeld, once told Brad Isaac [5], that the key to success in comedy was writing better jokes. He said that to accomplish this, you have to write every day. So, he told Brad to get a calendar and red marker and draw a big, red 'X' every day he wrote. "After a few days you'll have a chain. Just keep at it and the chain will grow longer every day. You'll like seeing that chain, especially when you get a few weeks under your belt. Your only job is to not break the chain."

"Don't break the chain," he said again for emphasis.

So, again, I ask you what your habits are? Not happy with your current habits? Here's a list of possible habits to pick up:

❖ Writing daily — Some recommend 1,000 words a day. Stephen King writes 2,000 words a day. It doesn't matter. Just write.

❖ Reading 10 pages daily—work or non-work-related

❖ Working out 30-40 mins per day

❖ Getting up earlier in the morning and having a *Miracle Morning* (Hal Elrod)

❖ Keeping a daily food journal through various available apps

❖ Looking at your finances daily

❖ Journaling one thing you are grateful for about your significant other daily

PUSH

Push it good. Push it real good. Ah, push it. Ah, push it.

— Salt-N-Pepa

* * *

Push yourself. Push yourself to your limit. Don't expect miracles. Don't expect handouts. Don't expect easy. Expect hard. Expect work. Expect long hours. Expect success.

Today I was listening to one of James Altucher's podcasts and his guest for the day was Gary Vaynerchuk. Gary talked about the classic dilemma everyone in the world experiences. Everyone wants the good life, but not everyone wants to work for it. Some people just want to sit on the couch watching *House of Cards*, or playing in their softball league, or just relaxing after getting home. Now, there's nothing wrong with those things, but you need to have your priorities straight. If you want the supposed good life, you won't get there by watching TV and wasting hours and hours of time doing nothing to take you to the next level.

Assuming you get off at 4 p.m. every day, you technically have 5-8 hours of free time—depending on when you go to bed. Since I love numbers, let's do some basic math. 5-8 hours per night working on your business gets you an additional 25-40 hours of work—not including the weekend. If you include weekends, you easily can add an additional 16+ hours. So, this gets us 41-56 hours of time spent on our business. Sound exhausting? So, is success. Add this time to your normal work schedule and you're working 81-96 hours/week. Forty-one extra hours per week gets us to 2,132 extra hours per year and 56 hours per week gets us to 2,912 extra hours per year.

Following the classic Malcolm Gladwell principle—it takes 10,000 hours of work to become an expert in your career field. Looking at our previous numbers, that gets us to 10,000 hours in 4.7 and 3.4 years, respectively. Not even a whole 5 years. No, it's not immediate gratification, but it's still damn fast. Stick at something—anything—for 3-4 years at 5-8 hours per day and you will become an expert.

Follow the principles of:

1. **Control your thoughts**
2. **Let the mind soar (imagination)**
3. **Use positivity and courage to define a goal**
4. **ACTION**

5. **Discipline — do it daily — never break the chain**

Your Greatest Enemy

People are where they are because that is exactly where they really want to be—whether they will admit that or not...Our mind returns what is planted. It doesn't care what is planted, though.

—Earl Nightingale

* * *

Control your thoughts. Your greatest enemy? Who is it? What about them makes your blood boil? Was it Carl from HR? Cynthia from Accounts Payable? Those A/P people are good at p*&%ing people off. No. Then, who is it? Go to the bathroom; turn the light on; look in the mirror. There they are. YOU, yourself, and I. Why aren't you as successful as you want? Why haven't you done more with your life? Why aren't you living the life you dream and desire? Because you created it.

Everything present or not present in your life is because of you. No one to blame. You can huff and puff until you're blue in the face. You're the only person responsible. If you can't even be honest with yourself about responsibility because step one is owning up to yourself. You have a shitty job because you made it so. You became this, that, or the other because you made it so.

Once you realize that you are where you are in life because you made it so, realize that your thoughts are the seedlings that got you there.

As Mahatma Gandhi says, "Your beliefs become your thoughts. Your thoughts become your words. Your words become your actions. Your actions become your habits. Your habits become your values. Your values become your destiny."

Action step: For the next week, wear a large rubber band around your wrist and carry a notebook with you. Listen to your self-talk. Every time you hear yourself doubting, bashing yourself, talking down to yourself, etc., snap the rubber band against your wrist and say something positive about yourself. Then, write it down. After the seven days are over, you will be surprised at how often you doubt, question, or beat down yourself. Learn positive self-talk. It takes time. Years of self-abuse don't become cured overnight.

2. Let the mind soar (imagination)

999 out of 1000 times—a ship will get to where it wants to go if it has a goal…No goals equals no purpose and having no direction to go. A lack of direction is the same as a lack of success.

—Earl Nightingale

What do you want? What do you really want out of life? The most important question you will EVER ask yourself. If you have no idea where you want to go, you will NEVER get there.

Cat: "Where are you going?
Alice: Which way should I go?
Cat: That depends on where you are going.
Alice: I don't know.
Cat: Then it doesn't matter which way you go."

— Lewis Carroll, *Alice in Wonderland*

If you don't figure out what you want out of life, no one else is going to do it for you.

Goals:

Things goals

Financial Goals

Personal development and work goals

Other (body and health, relationships, contribution, spirituality)

3. Use positivity and courage to define a goal

Action Step: Write down your top one to three goals every day. Write them each down in the present tense, e.g., "I earn $33,000 per month by December 2016." Or, "I self-published an Amazon #1 best-seller by April 30, 2016." Notice how these goals are also very concrete. Personally, I hate the phrase "SMART" goals, but the acronym gets its point across. Make goals that are specific, measurable, attainable, relevant, and time-bound. Do these goals pass the sniff test? Let's find out.

"I earn $33,000 per month by December 2016."

Specific: Yes, this goal is very specific and concrete. (What, why, who, where, which)

Measurable: Yes. How much? How many? Specific number or outcome?

Attainable: Maybe, but probably not. $33,000 per month is a drastic step up—assuming today's date is January 2016. $33,000 in 12 months is pushing this criteria.

Relevant: Yes. Does this goal matter to you? Does it bring up emotions and feelings within you?

Time-bound: Yes. December 2016. If you don't bind your goals, they are merely dreams or wishful thinking.

Let's look at the other example:

"I self-published an Amazon #1 bestseller by April 30, 2016."

Specific: Yes. Clear goal

Measurable: Yes. We know our criteria to achieve. #1 Amazon bestseller

Attainable: Yes. Assuming the person started January 1, they could have written 90,000 words if they wrote 1,000 words per day. Then, they spend the entire month of April editing, formatting, getting cover designs, and uploading their book.

Relevant: Yes. They've wanted this goal for over 7 years. It has meaning to them.

Time-bound: Yes. April 30, 2016. We know the benchmark and deadline.

4. ACTION

…He and his sane compositions never reach perfection, but are utterly eclipsed by the performances of the inspired madman.

The most important step of all. This is where we get to the real-talk. No more pussyfooting around the topics. Yes, we know that if you don't have goals, you obviously will never reach them. If you don't look at them every day and make them omnipresent everywhere in your life, you won't reach them either. But, I'm here to tell you that all the wishful thinking in the world, positive affirmations, or come-to-Jesus talks matter. None of it. As Arnold Schwarzenegger says, "If you want to win, there's absolutely no way around hard, hard work. None of my rules will bring success unless you do."

Work your ass off. No more dipping those baby-toes into the deep-end of the pool. Put your goggles on, close your eyes, and jump in. Open your eyes and realize that it wasn't so damn bad after that initial shock. Of course it hurts at first. Everyone feels that initial sting and pangs of discomfort. Push on. Put the effort in.

As we've mentioned earlier about the Jerry Seinfeld Productivity hack, whatever action you need to take—TAKE IT EVERY DAY. And when you do complete it every day, mark it off on the calendar or use an app to track your habits.

Find an accountability partner if you can't hold yourself accountable. What do coaches and mentors do? They hold you accountable. Why do so many people fail their New Year's Resolutions? Because no one is holding their feet to the fire and holding them accountable.

Action Steps: Every day, take one action toward your goals. Track them. If you can't hold yourself accountable and need that extra push, hire a coach or mentor in your chosen field. Most importantly, if you do hire one, DO NOT fire them when they hold you accountable. They are not your buddy. They are there to metaphorically kick you in your lazy, procrastinating ass when you stop moving.

Before you know it, your efforts will compound and your results will skyrocket.

Action —> Accountability —> Compound results

5.   Discipline — do it daily — never break the chain

The Strangest Secret in the World — An Homage to Earl Nightingale

We choose to go to the moon in this decade and do the other things. Not because they are easy, but because they are hard.

—John F. Kennedy

* * *

You think small. You get small. You think big. You get big. A cliché that is one of the most important concepts to live by.

Why are millionaires, multimillionaires, and billionaires more successful than you? Goals. Not just goals, but big goals. HUGE goals. One does not simply attain stratospheric success by little thinking or little living.

As we've talked about before and you've heard a million times before, goals are the key to your success. Yes, I'm sure you've heard it, but do you actively practice it? Do you sit down every day, write down your goals, visualize their attainment, and develop ways to assure their attainment? If not, then look around. Are you any closer to your dream life than before? Almost guaranteed, you are not.

Now, I won't beat the goal horse to death anymore, but an even more important idea is that of the *10X Rule* thinking, as Grant Cardone puts it. Stop thinking small and start thinking 10 times bigger and take 10X bigger actions.

The example he gives in the book is would you rather set a goal of making a $100,000 or $1,000,000 and suppose you fall short of your goal. For which goal would you rather fall short? $100,000 or $1,000,000? Some gurus tell you to pick the more realistic goal of $100,000 as part of the A in a SMART goal — attainable. Grant, however, advises against this small thinking. He says to use big thinking and big action. You can't expect to make a monstrous goal without taking even bigger action toward it.

For example, say you want to create a popular podcast or popular YouTube channel. Now depending on your content, (which varies) there are things you can control. One of the greatest things you control is your ability to control the volume of the content. You choose how often and when you distribute your content to listeners and viewers.

Now, some people might do weekly podcasts and some people might do weekly videos; however, if you want to apply 10X thinking to content distribution, think 10X bigger. Set a goal of DAILY content. Set a goal of making a DAILY podcast. Put in massive effort. Some of the most successful content providers out there are also the most consistent.

For example, a current successful YouTuber has 2,850 videos over a four year period. Let's do the math. 2,850 videos over a four year period is 712.5 videos/year. 712.5 videos/year is equivalent to 2 videos per day. Those are massive numbers. Even more impressive, are this person's YouTube stats. This person currently has 11,846,613 subscribers and 4,270,748,733 views. Yes, you read that right. Almost 4.3 billion views. Yes, with a capital 'B,' BILLION views.

Content matters. So does consistency. You control both. What do you choose? The moon or the sky?

Mr. President, thank you for choosing the moon.
—Bill Anders, Astronaut on Apollo 8

Learn to DREAM

Dream on…

—Aerosmith

* * *

Learn to DREAM. What does DREAM stand for? Rearrange the letters and you have the word, ARMED. Armed for what? For battle. If you're going to take on your dream(s), you need to be armed against yourself. As we say often—you are your greatest enemy.

1) **A ction**
2) **R ead**
3) **M editate**
4) **E ducation**
5) **D ream**

1. ACTION first.

Why first? Because it comes before everything else. You can dream and visualize and make affirmations until you turn blue in the face. None of them. I repeat. None of them work—unless you do.

Specifically, work your ass off. Let me take another step and emphasize the even more important point—work your ass off daily. DAILY ACTION. If we could all live by this mantra. This way of life. None of us would need to read self-help books, because we could help ourselves. And to really get to the heart of the matter, RELENTLESS DAILY ACTION. Don't just act. Don't just show up some of the time. Show up ALL THE TIME. Stop taking action whenever it feels good or convenient. Take action even when it's uncomfortable. Take action even when you've had zero sleep, dealt with assholes all day, and your day was a total bag-o-dicks.

I assure you that you will never read the phrase bag-o-dicks anywhere else. It's a metaphor...or something like that.

2. Read DAILY.

Preferably nonfiction. Not all books are created equally. If you enjoy fiction, I'm not telling you to quit fiction, but to simply add more nonfiction. As I mentioned earlier in the book, the more you read in your chosen career field the better you become at your job. The better you become at your job, the more money you earn. Read, rinse, repeat.

As Brian Tracy says in his book *Time Power*, "One hour a day translates into one book a week. One book a week translates into approximately fifty books over the next twelve months. If you read an hour a day, one book per week, you will be an expert in your field within three years. You will be a national authority in five years, and you will be an international authority in seven years."

Let's expand Mr. Tracy's example even further. Fifty books per year gets us to 250 books in five years. Even further out, 500 books read in just 10 years. Suppose you read 500 books in your chosen career field…you would be the foremost expert in any industry. I'm not sure some career fields even have 500 books in the entire world written about them. You very well may run out of books to read.   That's okay. At that point, you would be national authority and could write a book of your own on the topic.

The *Pew Research Center* stated [6], "The percentage of readers increased steadily as household income and education levels rose."

3. Meditate Daily — the missing link.

I consider this the missing link for high achievers. As we all know, many successful people are very good at putting more and more on their plate. What they are NOT always good at is keeping all those plates spinning. They may think they are, but it's not necessarily the tasks at hand that let you know that. Rather, it's your physiology. You may physically have everything under control. But, it's really what's under YOUR hood that matters most.

Several entrepreneurs I know push and push and push until they have drained every last mental, physical, and physiological resource in their body. They are running on empty constantly. What is a big, successful entrepreneur to do? Well, you should start by meditating daily. Now, there are many of you out there saying, "Oh, yeah I should meditate. Or, oh no, I don't have time for that." It doesn't matter either way. It matters. Period.

Now, there are also many, many types of meditation. There is Transcendental Meditation (TM) where you are giving a mantra. The downside, you pay $1000+ to learn how to meditate. Many well-known celebrities are big proponents of this style of meditation and swear by it. Others use a more present-state meditation—where you observe your breath and thoughts. Then, there's Buddhist meditation (Zen Meditation). Then, there are guided meditations. We also have Christian meditation.

The type doesn't matter. Find something that works for you and stick with it. Mind you, this doesn't need to be some big, dramatic process. This can be as simple or as complex as you make it. Most people, myself included, don't have hours upon hours to reflect on the meaning of life every day; however, I do have 10 minutes every day when I can practice mindfulness—more than enough to be at one with myself and center myself for the day.

The ideal time of day for meditation is early in the morning before work—when you can mentally set the tone for your day.

4. Education.

Many think education stops when you finish school. Nothing is farther from the truth. The minute you finish school—real education begins. In school, you didn't always get to choose the classes you wanted. School ends and you now have all the options in the world. What do you want to learn? Want to learn how to be a better speaker? Join a Toastmasters club. Want to be better at sales? Hire a coach or mentor.

Here's a magic bullet for you. Invest 10% of your income on education. Education is wide and varying. Books, coaches, mentors, seminars, conferences, audiobooks, training programs. You decide. What matters is that you decide to set aside 10% for these.

More ambitious? Be like the gentleman in the Brian Tracy book: *No Excuses! The Power of Self-Discipline.* At first he invested 3% of his $30,000 income to education. The next year his income raised to $50,000. That year, he invested 5% of his income on education. The next year his income passed $100,000. After that, he decided to really crank things up and invest 10% of his income. Where is he today? He now makes over one million dollars a year and still invests 10% of his income on education. Think about that?

Someone making $1,000,000/year invests $100,000 on education alone.

He spends more money on education than some people make in an entire year. How can you not expect someone like that not to keep growing? He will keep improving and evolving. The fellow sitting beside him with $0 invested in himself each year will stagnate. Learn to learn. Learning leads to leading. Leading leads to living.

Books like *Think and Grow Rich* have clever titles. Although, I agree with the original sentiments of the book, I think a better title would be **Learn and Grow Rich**. Yes, it matters what you want. If you don't know that—no one can help you. Though, once you know what you want, you have to learn how to get there. You learn two ways. One is failure. The other is education. The former can't necessarily be prevented. Everyone fails. The other is in your total control. Leverage it wisely.

5. Dream.

Know what you want. Why? Simple. Those who know what they want and dare to think about it daily—taking action all the while, eventually get to their destination. Maybe not immediately, but with enough effort, they get there.

When's the last time you wrote down your goals? Never. Time to change that. You can sit down and tell everyone around you about what you want, but it won't come true until you put it in writing and take ACTION.

If one had to give a weighted percentage on how important goals are compared to action, I would say 75% action to 25% goals. If you don't know what you want, you're never going to get there.

For example, I had a particular dream car on my list. I'm sure your dream car is different from mine, but my dream car was an Audi S5. Initially, I thought I was insane having such a dream car. Then, I realized that thankfully luxury European cars depreciate rapidly. Instead of the $60k sticker price, I bought one for well under one-third of that.

Dreams are a dangerous thing. Especially, if you do not take action. Inaction breeds a lack of confidence. A lack of confidence equates to a lack of goals achieved.

As Grant Cardone always says, use 10x thinking. 10x thinking leads to 10x action.

"The Slight Edge" by Jeff Olson

The Edge…There is no honest way to explain it because the only people who really know where it is are the ones who have gone over.

—Hunter S. Thompson

* * *

If you want to read a book that will change your life, this is one of them. And I've read hundreds of self-improvement books. This one ranks up there with the best of them. Jeff Olson discusses that everyday simple routines and rituals can make all the difference—or not—depending on if we actually complete them daily. He emphasizes how seemingly subtle and mundane tasks— that seem inconsequential can make all the difference.

In one of the most profound recommendations, he states we should read 10 pages of a book every day. Doing the math, 10 pages per day multiplied by 30 days in a month gives us 300 pages. 300 pages times 12 equals 3,600 pages. Assuming the average nonfiction book is 150 pages long, that will give you 24 books in one year—or 12 books if you like the thicker, 300-page books.

Or, take another example from Mr. Olson's book, exercising 35 minutes per day. He equates 35 minutes to about the same as reading 10 pages per day—just enough to make a big difference and not so much time that he neglects doing it. 35 minutes a day multiplied by 30 days in a month, equals 1,050 minutes times 12 months, equals 12,600 minutes ~210 hours. Think you could make massive improvements in your body composition with ~12,600 minutes in a year—absolutely.

What can you do daily in the following categories to make massive changes:

Relationships, health, wealth, finance, happiness, work, giving

The "Slight Edge" II — The Power of Numbers

Numbers constitute the only universal language.

—Nathanael West

* * *

Numbers are power. Compounded with—I'm a numbers nerd. Numbers are satisfying. There's nothing better than balancing and crunching numbers. It is definitive. It is concrete. No guessing. When you add numbers to self-improvement you get something even greater—change. I'm not talking New Year's Resolution change. I'm talking lasting change that will kick your ass and life.

Let's spitball some examples and figure out some activities we can use to prove our point. On the previous page, we talked specifically about reading and exercising. We used examples of the power of reading an extra 10 pages of a book in your career field every day and exercising 35 minutes per day—10 pages a day equals around 3,600 pages per year or 24 books at 150 pages a piece. And, exercising 35 minutes a day equals around 12,600 minutes per year.

In our new examples, let's choose some new options. Let's see here. How about relationships. As noted in the *Slight Edge*, the idea of writing down 365 reasons why you love your significant other—listing one reason each day.

As said many times before, the little things matter. The act of writing one reason why you appreciate your loved one each day takes so little time, it's a joke. Literally, it take 5-10 seconds to write down one reason. The challenge is staying consistent.

The act of writing down one reason for 365 days takes commitment. You can't pussy-foot around. Every day, like clockwork, you write down that reason. I don't care if you feel like shit, have a work project, don't feel like it, write that f$#&ing reason down. If you ever want to build discipline, you have to find something to do daily and keep doing it—DAILY.

It will seem completely inconsequential if you miss it one day; however, it is EVERYTHING. It's not even the act that matters. It could be whatever you decide. The thing that matters is doing that shit every day until you complete the task at hand. At the very least, I challenge you to try something for one year. Try writing, exercising, reading ten pages, or some other habit every day for the next year. If you actually make it an entire year, you will see how drastically your life has changed.

I challenge you. In fact, only 5%, if that, will take me up on my challenge. I would offer some kind of prize for completing this challenge, but then you are motivated to complete it because of an external source. The prize and reward is at the end of completing the task for an entire year. Words of advice: The greatest part of life is the journey, not the destination.

Addiction to Diction

Dic·tion ˈdikSH(ə)n/

Noun

1.   The choice and use of words and phrases in speech or writing.

* * *

Addiction is the new trend of our times. You name an addiction, we've got it—well, someone does: eating, sex, drugs, rock n' roll, rainbows, penguins, cats, dogs, eating rubber, porn, gambling, video games.

Why is addiction such a nasty f#$%@& to kick? Because in our little ape brains, chemicals fire off telling us that more of that something makes us feel good would make us feel even better. Naturally, we seek more of what makes us feel good and less of what makes us feel like shit. Why do we still do things that are harmful and cause us pain? Because the pleasure we get from doing it is greater than the sting of the pain. When the pain is greater than the pleasure, we're motivated to change our ways.

An example for you. I have a cousin who is addicted to video games. At one point in my life, I was in the same addiction cycle for 3-4 years. He, however, has been addicted to video games for 14 years. Yes, you heard me correctly, 14 years. To really give you an idea of how much he plays video games, I'm going to do some math for you. On average, if I had to guess, I'd say he plays games for around 10 hours per day—that's being conservative.

So, 365 days per year times 10 hours per day equals 3,650 hours per year and 51,110 hours over 14 years. The United States averaged 1,789 hours worked annually in 2014. My cousin in comparison has worked the equivalent of 28.5 years playing video games over a 14 year period. Yes, you heard that correctly, it would take the average U.S. citizen 28.5 years (working 1,789 hours each year) to have worked 51,110 hours. Addiction? You're fucking right. Consistent? Give my cousin a fucking award for being the most consistent person in the world.

Rain or shine, without question, my cousin will continue his addiction. What benefit does he get? He gets the stimulus of entertainment and social interaction through the internet. What doesn't he get? He doesn't get real, live social interaction. He has social anxiety, hasn't held a real job, women are repulsed by him, still lives at home, and feels absolutely shitty about his life.

It makes me cringe even talking about him, because I have been in his shoes. Addiction is a bastard. Some addictions are worse than others; however, they all change our neural pathways. The more indulge in them. The more we need them to get to our baseline. Is it possible for him to kick 14 years of playing video games 10 hours a day? Yes, but it will be quite the undertaking. Don't let yourself become my cousin. Not even close.

Prolific Proliferation

I'm barely prolific and incredibly lazy.

—Tom Petty

* * *

Want to be a person that constantly garners the attention of others? Want to make all of your wildest dreams come true? Want to be the envy of those around you? Become a person of principles. Don't just strive to do something every so often or every couple days. Strive to obliterate what you're doing. If you're a writer that currently writes 300 words per day, write 3,000 words; Stephen King writes 2,000 words per day. Just imagine writing more than someone selling more than 350 million books and a net worth estimated at $400 million.

Many think there is some mystery to success. There is not. There never was. Why do they put your income to shame? They outwork you. That's it. You are lazy. Or, maybe there's some of you out there saying, "I'm not lazy, you asshole." Apologies. You aren't consistent. That's better. While other successful people show up every day, you show up when you feel like it. Rain, shine, or snow. They're there. Guess what? They don't always want to show up—just like you. The difference? They put their shoes on one foot at a time and lace up—preparing themselves for the grind.

Become a grinder. When you grind, you gain. Don't let someone else outwork you. If nothing else, become a person with a work ethic. Never let someone put in more hours or time. Put in more hours on the weekend than most put in at their full-time job. This is just as much advice for you as it is me. If I'm going to go down in flames, I better at least give a good effort.

Grind to gain. Be prolific.

Mindset

The Bob Ross Analogy

Let's paint a happy little tree.

—Bob Ross

* * *

This isn't necessarily an analogy about Bob Ross; it just happened to have a catchy title; however, the analogy is about paint. So, I suppose, in a sense, they are relatable.

The other day, I was painting a backdrop for my photography business. I noticed one thing. The color white took twice as much paint to get good coverage. Black paint only took two coats. Then, when I cleaned out the paint from the brushes and rollers, I noticed the white paint tended to stick around longer than the black paint. For the most part, I could get rid of the majority of the black paint, but the white paint stayed around.

This made me think about habits and rituals in life. In life, good habits seem very difficult to adopt and stick. We have the best of intentions at the beginning of each new year—exercising, eating healthier, running—for the first week or so. Then, as time progresses, we gradually begin to slip until we've altogether given up. At best, we may make it a month. At worst, we last less than a week.

Just like the white paint when applying to the backdrop, it took more layers to finally stick. Good habits and rituals take more time to develop than vices and bad habits. It is far easier to pick up bad habits—TV, junk food, video games, drugs, alcohol.

Though, once you develop these good habits, they tend to stick more than vices do. In my opinion, it is far harder to develop good habits than it is to rid yourself of bad ones. Some would disagree with that statement, but I disagree with them. Taking away something—anything—is easier than it is to add something.

Bad habits form more quickly than good habits. Good habits have more stickability than bad habits.

Your bad habits: watching three hours of television every day, smoking a pack of cigarettes a day and eating like shit. What happens when you take these vices away? You have three hours of free time every day to fill with, less smoking at work, more money in your pockets, and getting rid of every bad food choice you've made.

You'll have a harder time replacing these bad habits with good ones. Remember, it's easier to eradicate a bad habit than develop a positive one.

Replace those 3 hours of television with several hours of learning something new, exercising, cooking. Yes, it will be uncomfortable. Yes, it will take time to develop a new routine. Yes, you will make it out alive.

The Little Voice Inside Your Head

If you hear a voice within you say, "You cannot paint," then by all means paint and that voice will be silenced.

—Vincent van Gogh

* * *

You know the voice. The voice that says you can't. You won't. You shouldn't. You're not worthy. Around every little corner, destroying your decisions with indecision. Why do we constantly punish ourselves? It all comes down to self-preservation.

The human body is very good at resiliency and surviving—not nearly as good at pushing its limits mentally. Or, rather, it's harder to push its limits. It feels more difficult to expand mentally than it does physically. Yes, the physical is hard as well, but destroying limiting beliefs is, in effect, destroying a part of who you are. You are destroying the old you, the part that no longer has a role.

I think even more important is finding a way to silence the negativity. It isn't even so much about being positive all the time. It isn't about positivity. Positivity 100% of the time is mental masturbation. The real key is merely silencing the shit talking side of you. As long as you can silence that side, all is well in the world. Instead of saying you can't do something, you're just not saying anything.

The way to achieve this—a rubber band. Every time you hear that voice come up, put a rubber band around your wrist and snap your wrist. The key is cognizance and being aware and present of your thoughts. The more you do this routine, the more you become aware of your thought patterns. The more aware you are, the more likely it is to destroy your shitty self-talk.

Will it ever go away completely? Probably not. We are human, after all. Will it help? Yes.

Also, read: *The Power of Now* by Eckhart Tolle.

You Are Not Your Thoughts

Deep within man dwell those slumbering powers; powers that would astonish him, that he never dreamed of possessing; forces that would revolutionize his life if aroused and put into action.

—Orison Swett Marden

* * *

Something profound to realize. Every thought running through your head is not you. Yes, you may think it, but you are not your thoughts; you are the observer. Instead of thinking that you are your thoughts. Realize that you are one step above that. Here's what I mean. When you hear something, you think it is you, but it's not. For example, random thoughts constantly pop up in your head, "I'm scared of this. I can't do that." But, when you think about it, what or who is telling you that? Is it you?

Yes and no. In a sense, it is you. It is your subconscious trying to preserve itself. As I've said before, our bodies and minds are created for self-preservation.

Our previous ancestors, had to worry about merely existing. Today, that may be true for some, but not most. So, our primordial pea-brains never evolved in that sense. We treat scary scenarios as if we are risking our very existence. We aren't. Which is why it feels so goddamn difficult to overcome fears. We are quite literally going against everything programmed into our brains. We basically have to short-circuit the system and realize that we won't die from fear or failure.

The greatest asset in life is not listening to yourself—and you are the hardest person to ignore. You need to evolve. You need to listen. Listen to what? Yourself. Every day take time to meditate. Start with ten minutes. During those ten minutes, see what thoughts arise. Thoughts come in waves. One minute you think about this; another minute you think about that. Learn to acknowledge the thoughts. Listen. Listen like a doctor would to a patient—with open ears.

Realize that you are not your thoughts. Your thoughts do not determine your future. Your actions define you. Learn to listen to the entity between your ears and acknowledge it has thoughts, but do not necessarily believe everything that it tells you at face value. All it knows is how to survive.

The Power of Negative Thinking

Your world is a living expression of how you are using and have used your mind.

— Earl Nightingale

* * *

Every day for the next 7 days, write 3 things you are ungrateful for.

❖ Also, write down at least one person you are mad at each day.

❖ If someone wrongs you, think of ways to plot your revenge.

❖ Think about all the things you don't have and why you don't deserve them.

❖ Think about your past and how you haven't lived your dream life.

❖ Think about your future and why you won't have what you want.

❖ Think about your current situation and blame others.

❖ Think about your current situation and reasons why you can't have your dream life.

❖ Think about all of your self-limiting beliefs all day, every day.

❖ Mentally beat yourself up over all the ways you are inadequate and don't deserve the good life.

❖ Be jealous of those that have what you don't.

❖ Gossip about others.

❖ Talk poorly about rich people and those that have what you don't.

❖ List all the ways you are poor.

Good. Now, that we've called out what you have been doing, let's look at some alternatives.

❖ Every day for the next 7 days, write 3 things you appreciate

❖ Write down at least one person you love each day.

❖ If someone wrongs you, consider ways to forgive them.

❖ Think about all the things you don't have and why you DO deserve them.

❖ Think about your future and how you to live your dream life.

❖ Think about your future and what you want.

- ❖ Think about your current situation and take personal responsibility for where you are in life.

- ❖ Think about your current situation and reasons why you can have your dream life.

- ❖ Think about all of your strengths. All day, every day.

- ❖ Use affirmations declaring why you are powerful beyond measure and deserve the good life.

- ❖ Bless and admire those that have what you don't.

- ❖ Don't gossip about others.

- ❖ Talk positively about rich people and those that have what you don't.

- ❖ List all the ways you are rich.

Good Vibrations

I'm pickin' up good vibrations…Good, good, good, good vibrations.

—Beach Boys

* * *

Good vibrations. Good, good vibrations. This section is about the power of positive intentions. Rather, positive beliefs. Many books are out there about the power of positive thinking. As we talked about before, imagine what your ultimate desires are vis-à-vis your goals. Once you create your goals, use positive intentions, and most importantly—MASSIVE action.

This section, however, is strictly about positive intentions—not goals or taking action. Though, it is important to note that you lose vast efficacy by only using one of the above three steps. Just like The Three Musketeers—"One for all, and all for one." Or, as Alexandre Dumas originally penned the term, "Un pour tous, tous pour un."

Here is the most important bit to take away from this section. Your mind is like a lightning rod. Anything you think about will attract more of it into your life. Think negative, get more negative. Think positive, get more positive. I'm sure you know people that embody the negative form of this all the time. Phrases like, "I'm just not lucky." Or, "I'll never be rich." Or, "I'll never be skinny." Whatever their limiting belief is, they make it true. The more you tell yourself these things, the more they become true and the more verification shows up in your life.

Conversely, think about times where you've told yourself the opposite. "I'm a great [fill in the blank]." "I'm a good public speaker." "I'm a good friend." The only difference is your belief. You believe you are x, y, or z. Change your thinking. Change your beliefs. Change your beliefs. Change your life.

Delusional? No. Maybe fake it 'til you make it. To me, I'd rather be an overconfident fake instead of an unconfident sham. Everyone starts out at the bottom of any skill or job, but it doesn't mean you stay there. You just need to believe you already have the mindset of the next level. Mentally become what you desire to manifest. Feel what it would feel like. Visualize what you look like. Experience the emotional polarity with the future you. How do you feel? How do you look?

Recap: Your mind is like a lightning rod. Whatever thoughts that come about, will promulgate more of the same. Think positive thoughts. Get positive thoughts. Think negative thoughts. Get negative thoughts.

Number two: Take great confidence in your imagination. Don't let your past or present self dissuade you from striving boldly. Dare to reach further. Expand your reach of your goals. See how far you can go.

It takes courage to be the person you dream about. It takes even more courage to be the person other people envy. Dare to dream bigger.

Exercise: As we did previously, wear a large rubber band around your wrist for the next week or longer. I recommend wearing one until you can consciously observe your thoughts and stop negative thoughts at the source. Until you become a master of your mind, you will be a slave to every vagary thought. The minute you think negatively of yourself, or tell yourself you can't do something, smack your wrist with the rubber band and replace that thought with something positive. We are teaching ourselves that negative thoughts or pessimism no longer binds our realities. We will no longer tolerate this thinking.

Number three: The naysayers. Once you've mastered your own thinking, you must regulate others around you. Unfortunately, those around us with the best of intentions also, at times, give the worst advice. If we don't shatter our own dreams, there's always a trusty friend or relative to knock us down a notch. Some are conscious attempts at knocking us down—others meant with the best intentions.

You have to remember that these are your dreams and yours alone. They don't matter to anyone other than yourself. Hold them closely. The best course of action is keeping it sacred and telling no one. Hold that dream close. Don't talk about it. Do it. Action talks. Bullshit walks. Let them hate on you after you're already miles ahead and they see your afterburners.

The best analogy you will ever hear on life, your dreams, and how others (will) react to your dreams:

"Crabs in a bucket" [7]

> *"Crab mentality is a phrase popular among Filipinos, and was first coined by writer Ninotchka Rosca, in reference to the phrase crabs in a bucket. It describes a way of thinking best explained by the phrase "If I can't have it, neither can you." The metaphor refers to a pot of crabs.*

Individually, the crabs could easily escape from the pot, but instead, they grab at each other in a useless "king of the hill" competition which prevents any from escaping and ensures their collective demise. The analogy in human behavior is that members of a group will attempt to "pull down" (negate or diminish the importance of) any member who achieves success beyond the others, out of envy, conspiracy or competitive feelings.

This concept figures prominently in Terry Pratchett's novel "Unseen Academicals." A fish monger does not bother to keep a lid on the crab bucket because "any that try to get out get pulled back." The protagonist comes to realize that his social status results not from external repression, but from his own low expectations of himself: "The worst of it is, the crab that mostly keeps you down is you."

Drive 150

I can't drive fifty-five.

—Sammy Hagar

* * *

Stop pussyfooting around. Life doesn't reward the slow lane. Who's in the slow lane you ask? Prius, Fiats, mom vans. Sure they're economical. They're safe. They're the logical choice. Does that sound like you? Does that sound like the kind of person you want to be? I hope not. If it does, stop reading now.

Life rewards those that go fast enough without losing control. Those that drive 55 end up exactly where you see them—in the right lane. For those of you left-laners...I offer a different choice. Sunglasses on. Engine revving the tach at redline—screaming and begging for that next gear—hoping you push it further—letting it breathe that sweet, cold air into its intake. 65. 75. 85. 105. 125. 150. Where do you pullback? Where do you lose control?

The higher you perform at each speed, the more speed you can handle. You keep progressing until you lose control or you back off on the gas pedal. As much as you want to blame other drivers around you for limiting your speed—only you decide that. Realize that your speed is decided entirely by you and you alone.

The minute you realize that you are in total control of your speed, you shift your actions. If you want to get somewhere quicker (in life), you better speed up—or watch everyone else pass you by.

Speed has never killed anyone…Suddenly becoming stationary—
that's what gets you.

—Jeremy Clarkson, Host of *Top Gear*.

The Fuck It List

I don't always recommend it, but at certain times of your life you've got to quit being such a slave to your pussiness and step up and see how well you can do under shitty conditions.

—Jim Wendler

* * *

Compliments of the Navy SEAL (David Goggins) from the book *Living With a Seal* by Jesse Itzler.

I've seen many, many people mention the bucket list—popularized by the movie appropriately titled, The Bucket List. However, I've seen even fewer name the exact opposite—The Fuck It List. Of the few Fuck It lists I've seen, it's usually the same. Their list is a list of items that they will no longer do or tolerate.

Instead, I challenge you to create a fuck it list of things that you don't want to do and DO THEM. Every day, you should—no, you must—do something that makes you uncomfortable. Try doing something that makes you grow—that makes you expand yourself and your comfort zone.

Life isn't meant to be comfortable. In fact, life is pretty goddamn difficult if you don't have your head down with the eye on the prize. Life is the ultimate equalizer.

Weightlifters often say the barbell is the ultimate equalizer. The barbell being a metaphor for life. In life, you will become weighed down many, many times. What matters isn't how many times you're weighed down, but how many times you get yourself back up.

Action Items:

Create a list now of the 10 things that you absolutely don't want to do—things that you're terrified of doing.

Example List:

- ❖ Speaking in public
- ❖ Dancing
- ❖ Skydiving
- ❖ Creating your own business
- ❖ Writing a book
- ❖ Coaching
- ❖ Learning a new sport
- ❖ Failing

- ❖ Swimming with sharks
- ❖ Going to a foreign country and speaking with locals

HUMOR

Email Wars: Uncivil War

I love the smell of napalm in the morning.

—Lt Col Bill Kilgore, *Apocalypse Now*

* * *

Email wars. Not all are created equally. There is something intoxicating about the metaphorical katanas flying through the inter-webs as keyboard jockeys and one-upness ensues. Now, without further ado, I present to you email modern warfare.

Webster's Dictionary War — when people argue over the correct interpretation of something, e.g., in regulation 5, paragraph 2.1, it states that such and such. To which they reply, "Well, in regulation 2, paragraph 6.7, it contradicts regulation 5, paragraph 2.1." A true battle of the minds.

The Passive Aggressive Email — when someone emails you and indirectly accuses you of not doing something, i.e., "Hey, have you by chance seen that email I sent you yesterday afternoon that I sent immediately after the workday ended?"

The Aggressive Email — When someone no longer has an ounce of respect left for you they will outright textually abuse you. A good rule of thumb—the shorter the email, the more aggressive it is. If they send you an abusive email in the length of a "love letter," they obviously don't do shit at work. The best response to a lengthy abuse is one of two options—no response or a short response.

An example that our friend Steve received the other week:

"Stev (they intentionally misspelled his name to be a dick),

Last week I emailed you about processing my leave pay—to which you have not replied. I am fully aware you are all busy over there in Finance, but I have some bills coming due and need this money. I would appreciate if you would reply back to me and at least have the courtesy to answer a question...Because, the last time I checked, your job is to answer customer concerns. I don't want to, but if I need to, I will get my supervisor involved to get the ball rolling. If that doesn't work, I will get my commander involved.

Thank you in advance for your reply."

Steve replies back with the following email:

"Sir,

OK.

-Steve"

<u>Total Domination Email</u> — my new favorite email war. This email is all-out warfare. They are rare, but when they happen, you know you've witnessed something special. It happens when someone sends out one of those emails with 50+ recipients. Within the email, they say something ignorant or blatantly wrong. So, someone gets the balls to "reply to all" and call that person out. Then, if you are lucky enough to see the unicorn email, the original sender will "reply to all" with a snarky comment of their own. To you gentlemen, I thank you for including me in something magical.

The Oopsie-daisy — when someone accidentally talks shit about someone via email, e.g., "Did you see that horrible dress Karen was wearing today? #trainwreck." To which Karen replies, "At least I'm not a fat bitch that talks behind someone's back." We're on your side, Karen. Debra is a backstabbing whore.

The Email Chain Ball-Drop — when someone emails 50 people—saying, "See attached."—and there's no attachment. Immediately followed with an email with the aforementioned attachment. Thanks for clogging my inbox, a-hole. Get it right the first time.

Under the See — when someone forwards something to you and they simply say, "See below." I like the effort, Jeffrey. You could at least summarize what the five f#$%ing paragraphs below are—dick.

**See Chapter 1 about why emails are better than phone calls. (documentation)

Epilogue

Job Satisfaction: The Man, The Myth, The Lie

I can't get no satisfaction.

—Mick Jagger

* * *

Are you happy with your job? According to a report by the *Conference Board*, [8] in 2014, 52.3% of Americans are unhappy with their job. Every year since 1987, the Board has run a job satisfaction survey. The nadir came 2010, when 57.4% of workers were unhappy with their jobs. Again, I ask you, are you happy with your job?

Now, there are several factors that make someone happy at work: money, meaningful work, interesting work, and their co-workers. Factoring all of these, the two most important are meaningful work and your co-workers.

Of all the factors, co-workers are the single-most important factor of job satisfaction. For example, I have a co-worker that is determined to work in another office because of the money. She wants that extra chunk of change—gosh darn it. "It's my money, and I want it right MEOW!" Granted, where she would work is filled with wonderful people; however, this is not always the case. Other people aren't so lucky. Some people move offices, jobs, and companies, all in pursuit of the next big thing. Now, there is absolutely nothing wrong with wanting to make more money—but, and it's a big BUTT (big booty Judy, big). Are you selling your soul to make a dollar?

For the love of god, do not take a job that you don't/won't enjoy, with people you don't like, at a company that only gives a shit about the bottom line, and end up working 100 hours per week. Suppose you make $100,000/year. There are 52 weeks in the year and let's assume you work 40-hour workweeks. 40 times 52 equals 2080 hours worked per year. $100,000/year divided by 2080 hours equals $48/hour. Now, let's assume that you work 70 hours per week. 52 weeks times 70 hours per week equals 3640 hours worked per year. $100,000/year divided by 3640 hours equals $27/hour.

Lessons to take away: Don't trade your time for money. And, if you do, do something you love. More than likely, it might not be at a traditional job. So, you might need to start your own business. Scary? Maybe. Just remember that the only job security is the job security you create.

As Jim Carrey's dad told him, "I learned many, many lessons from my father, but not the least of which is that you can fail at something you don't want, so you might as well take a chance doing what you love."

The Ending — Or the Beginning

> Spend each day trying to be a little wiser than you were when you woke up. Discharge your duties faithfully and well. Step by step you get ahead, but not necessarily in fast spurts. But you build discipline by preparing for fast spurts. Slug it out one inch at a time, day by day. At the end of the day – if you live long enough – most people get what they deserve.

> — Charlie Munger

* * *

One of the most powerful Super Bowl commercials of all time was from [9] Monster.com. As a child, you thought in terms of limitlessness. Nothing was impossible.

When someone asked you what you wanted to be, you knew and said it with pride. "I want to be an astronaut." "I want to be a

pilot." "I want to be a race car driver." "I want to be a dancer."
What happened? People told you to be realistic. Stop dreaming.
You need a real job. They killed your dreams. They defined who
and what you could become.

The Monster commercial asks kids what they want to be when
they grow up. Instead of the usual answers, they respond with
something oddly familiar…

"When I grow up—I want to file
all day."

"Climb my way up to middle
management."

"Be replaced on a whim."

"I want to have a brown nose."

"I want to be a yes man."

"Yes woman."

"Yes sir. Coming sir."

"Anything for a raise, sir."

"When I grow up, I want to be
under-appreciated."

"Be paid less for doing the same
job."

"I want to be forced into early retirement."

Ending with the powerful question: "What did you want to be?"

Did the child you were become the man or woman you are today?

I leave you with the question:

"WHAT DO YOU WANT TO BE?"

Once you know what you want, you learn the how by ACTING.

It is not the critic who counts;
nor the man who points out how the
strong man stumbled, or where the
doer of deeds could have done them
better. The credit belongs to the man
who is actually in the arena, whose
face is marred by dust and sweat and
blood; who strives valiantly; who errs
and comes short again and again; who

knows the great enthusiasms, the great devotions and spends himself in a worthy course; who at the best, knows in the end the triumph of high achievement, and who, at worst, if he fails, at least fails while daring greatly; so that his place shall never be with those cold and timid souls who **know neither victory or defeat**.

—Theodore Roosevelt

References

1. Tracy, Brian. Time Power: A Proven System for Getting More Done in Less Time than You Ever Thought Possible. New York: AMACOM, 2004. Print.

2. Leubsdorf, Ben. "We're Working More Hours—and Watching More TV." The Wall Street Journal. N.p., 24 June 2015. Web. 20 Jan. 2016.

3. "Average Annual Hours Actually Worked Per Worker." Organization For Economic Co-operation and Development. N.p., n.d. Web. 20 Feb. 2016.

4. "Index Fund Definition | Investopedia." Investopedia. N.p., 20 Nov. 2003. Web. 3 Mar. 2016.

5. Trapani, Gina. "Jerry Seinfeld's Productivity Secret." Lifehacker. N.p., 24 July 2007. Web. 26 Jan. 2016.

6. Rainie, Lee, and Maeve Duggan. "Overview." Pew Internet Libraries RSS. N.p., 27 Dec. 2012. Web. 23 Feb. 2016.

7. Vibes, John. ""Crabs In A Bucket" As An Analogy For Modern Human Society." True Activist. N.p., 19 Aug. 2015. Web. 2 Dec. 2015.

8. Adams, Susan. "Most Americans Are Unhappy At Work." Forbes. Forbes Magazine, 20 June 2014. Web. 2 Mar. 2016.

9. "Monster.com - "When I Grow Up"" YouTube. YouTube, 25 Feb. 2008. Web. 18 Apr. 2016.

www.ingramcontent.com/pod-product-compliance
Lightning Source LLC
Chambersburg PA
CBHW070327190526
45169CB00005B/1782